THE BOOK OF REVELATION

The late Dr. G. K. A. Bell, Bishop of Chichester, wrote:

"J. B. Phillips completes his translation of the New Testament with the Revelation of St. John. It is admirable. There is no lessening of the mystery, but the version is written in so clear and vivid a style that the reader cannot fail to be entranced and enthralled. And what gives him quite special assistance in his understanding of the book is the aptness and frequency of the sub-titles with which the different sections or paragraphs are introduced."

Religious Books in the Fontana Series

The Book of Revelation

A new translation of the Apocalypse

J. B. PHILLIPS

COLLINS

fontana books

First published 1957
First issued in Fontana Books 1960

To all those hopeful and encouraging people who for many years have urged me to undertake this work

Printed in Great Britain
Collins Clear-Type Press: London and Glasgow

CONTENTS

TRANSLATOR'S PREFACE

The book of Revelation, entitled in the Authorised Version "The Revelation of Saint John the Divine", was probably originally entitled, "A Revelation of John". Books of revelation, or apocalypses, were common in Jewish literature in times of national persecution, and this Christian apocalypse closely follows the form and style of such writings. Yet the claim made at the very beginning of the book is startling and unique—it is no less than "a revelation of Jesus Christ which God gave Him", and which was disclosed to John through an angelic intermediary. Although there was much argument and hesitation before this book was established within the canon of the New Testament, the historic fact is that from about the fifth century onwards the Western Churches at least accepted this book as uniquely inspired. I have therefore felt justified in giving this translation of the work the title of *The Book of Revelation.*

Although the majority of Christians quite cheerfully accept the inclusion of this mysterious book within the New Testament canon, my strong impression is that very few of them have read it in any detail. Most Christians, for example, are familiar with the Messages to the Seven Churches contained in the first three chapters, and know something of the closing two chapters of the book with their strangely haunting visions of the Holy City, the New Heaven and the new earth, and the strong promises of God to the faithful believer. But the intervening chapters remain puzzling and baffling to many sincere Christians. The form and idiom of apocalyptic writing is exceedingly strange to modern minds, and while the queer visions provide every opportunity for the diversion of cranks and fanatics, the sober Christian soon finds himself at a loss to understand, and in consequence frequently neglects the book completely.

I was naturally tempted to omit this book altogether from my translational work, a course, incidentally, taken by Calvin in his New Testament commentary. But this would lead to the obvious implication that I was taking it upon myself to exclude this work from the New Testament! Admittedly there have been times when I have sympathised with Martin Luther in his declaration that this book is "neither apostolic nor prophetic", that "everyone thinks of the book whatever his spirit suggests" and even "that there are many nobler books to be retained". Yet after much study I became satisfied that the Christian Church was justified in including this book in the Sacred Canon.

Eventually I began the translation of this book for two reasons, and I think that the results of my work may prove surprising. My first and obvious reason for doing the work at all is because I naturally wanted to complete my study, as well as my translation, of the whole New Testament. Like many another Christian I knew this book only superficially. My hope was that just as the essential truth of the Gospels and Epistles sprang to fresh life in the process of translation, so new truth and understanding would break upon me as I attempted to turn this peculiar Greek into modern English. This hope has not been altogether fulfilled, partly because my own method of translation, which is suitable enough for the narrative of the Gospels and the Acts, and to the epistolary style of Paul and the others, does not appear to lend itself to translating language which is both symbolic and poetic, and could easily lose both beauty and significance when reduced to a workaday vocabulary.

Nevertheless it soon became clear that, although the task was not the same as it had been in the other parts of the New Testament, it could prove useful and even, in the true sense of that threadbare word, thrilling. For in this book the translator is carried into another dimension—he has but the slightest foot-hold in the Time-and-space world with which he is familiar. He is carried, not into some never-never land of fancy, but into the Ever-ever land of God's eternal Values and Judgments. It is true that the expressions are often conventionally apocalyptic, but the translator can hardly fail to sense the urgency of the Seer as he tries to express the inexpressible. Surely something of the sense of timelessness, the feeling of the supra-mundane, can be conveyed? At least the language can be freed from archaisms and some verbal obscurities, and made more like that which a modern mystic might wish to use in setting down a series of burning instants of Heavenly vision.

As the character of the task became clearer to me I thought of my second reason for undertaking the translation—which is simply that a great many people have written asking me to do so! I think that for them, as for me, there lies something of a surprise. For I am pretty sure that those who found the obscurities of Paul's Epistles dissipated by the plain English of *Letters to Young Churches* will expect the obscurities of the book of Revelation to be dispersed by the same method. But quite plainly the cause of obscurity in Paul's letters is not the same as in John's apocalypse. In the case of Paul there is rarely any real doubt as to what his original intention was, complicated and compressed though his expressions sometimes are. It is comparatively easy by using imaginative insight, a little expansion and occasionally a little paraphrase, to turn into modern English his inspired thoughts of nearly two thousand years ago. But in the book of Revelation the obscurity is of a different and much more impenetrable quality. Who can truly translate unless he is quite sure of the original meaning? Who can explain or expand if both mystery and compression are felt to be an essential part of the original writing? If the author intends a mystery, then the translator must transmit a mystery; if the author is deliberately obscure the translator can only reproduce the obscurity!

If, then, my friends who have written to me so encouragingly and hopefully, are expecting the sort of detailed explanation which only a commentary can supply, or speculate about, they will not find it here in this work of translation. I must simply refer them to the Commentaries listed on page 21. But if they will read the whole of this mysterious book in the English of today, and allow its awe-inspiring sweep and compass to affect them as it affected me, they may be surprised but I do not think they will be disappointed.

. . . .

Now although I do not possess the special knowledge required in a commentator on apocalyptic, I feel it is legitimate and indeed might prove useful to record something of my impressions as a translator. The most obvious and striking feature of the book at first sight is the oddness of the Greek in which it is written. The differences of style and composition between the various books of the New Testament is completely hidden for most English readers by the overall majesty of the Authorised Version. (Indeed it is doubtful whether any difference in the style of writing between any of the New Testament books could be detected if one worked from the Authorised Version alone. The actual difference in style between, let us say, Luke's Gospel and Paul's Epistle to the Romans is very marked and, like other modern translators, I have made some attempt to reproduce this difference in the mode of translation.) But when one is confronted with the language of Revelation it is no mere difference of style which makes one gasp, but crudities, grammatical errors and a quite extraordinary juxtaposition of words. So wholly different is the book in its word-usage and composition from the Fourth Gospel that many scholars find themselves unable to believe that both could be written by the same person. The Fourth Gospel is written, within its limited vocabulary, smoothly and correctly and would probably have caused no literary qualms in a contemporary Greek reader. But Revelation piles word upon word remorselessly, mixes cases and tenses without apparent scruple, and shows at times a complete disregard for normal syntax and grammar. Here, for example, are a few words from chapter 8, verse 13, translated literally, representing roughly the appearance such Greek would present to an educated reader of the first century:

> And I saw, and I heard one eagle flying in mid-heaven saying in a loud voice,
> "Alas, alas, alas for the inhabitants upon the earth from the remaining voices of the
> trumpet of the three angels about to sound the trumpet!"

And such an example could be multiplied again and again. But, generally speaking, the tumultuous assault of words is not without its effect upon the mind, although I must confess I find it very difficult to believe that such a surprising attack could have been deliberately engineered. The inspired words seem to me to pour forth in a stream both uninhibited and uncorrected, and I therefore find it impossible to agree with those who say that this work is either a revision of an earlier one or a combination of several such works. The writer's mind was plainly steeped in the spirit and in the knowledge of Jewish apocalyptic. There is hardly a single direct quotation from the Old Testament but there are scores of parallels, echoes and recollections of it. John's words give the strong impression of one whose thoughts and thought-forms are Hebrew, and yet it is a puzzle to understand why such a keen and intelligent mind could not readily have mastered the simple usages of New Testament Greek. I make therefore this bold suggestion: that the writer, who had a genuine ecstatic experience, wrote down what he saw *during the visions*. The intense emotion of being, as it were, "in the heavenlies", the excitement of seeing what is normally invisible to human eyes, and the frustration of having to use human words to describe what is beyond human expression would, it seems to me, fully account for the incoherence, the strange formation of sentences, the repetition and the odd juxtaposition of words. If we suppose this to be true and if we suppose also that the writer were wholly convinced that what he had written was in fact written while "in the spirit", then we can reasonably imagine that he would shrink from correction or revision lest he distort or modify the revelation he had been given.

I feel I must record that, once one has absorbed the initial shock of the peculiar Greek, the effect of the language of this book is most powerful.

The crowns, the thrones, the gold, the jewels, the colours, the trumpets, the violence of action and the impact of incredible numbers and awe-inspiring size—all these images stir that threshold of the brain where monsters lurk and supernatural glories blaze. John is stirring with a kind of surrealistic artistry the vastnesses of our unconscious minds. The book is probably an impossibility for the pictorial illustrator, but the figures created in the mind are vivid and powerful enough to transport us to another spiritual dimension. Once we are gripped by the mysterious compulsion of these visions we find the "silence in Heaven for what seemed to be about half-an-hour" almost intolerable. The "solitary eagle flying in mid-air", crying out in pity for the inhabitants of the earth is, out of its context, bizarre to the point of absurdity, but, set as it is, it is almost unbearably poignant. And how beautifully right, how poetically satisfying it is to read that the leaves of the Tree of Life in the New Jerusalem are for the healing of the nations! The poetic impact of the book carries us away to a realm where the pedestrian rules of grammar no longer apply—we are dealing with celestial poetry and not with earthly prose. To be literal-minded and studiously analytical in such a work is to kill its poetic truth. Dissection is not infrequently the death of beauty.

I am conscious, then, of not having done much beyond removing some of the obscurities of archaic language. If there is any truth in my surmise that John was reluctant to alter or improve the messages he wrote down in ecstasy, then the reader will understand my own even greater reluctance to demolish the high poetry of these strange utterances by reducing them to the language of everyday experience. Almost any poem can be made to look ridiculous by having its superficial meaning reduced to ordinary prose. (We have only thus to "translate" Keats' "Ode on a Grecian Urn" or Shelley's "To a Skylark" to see how easily the magic and mystery can be destroyed!) This by no means proves that a poem is bad poetry; on the contrary it emphasises the proper use of poetry which, by indefinable subtleties of rhythm, rhyme and cadence, can strike chords and overtones forever beyond the reach of the finest prose. Consequently my earnest hope is that the use of modern language has not quenched the flame which blazes through this magnificently ecstatic poem of the Majesty and Sovereignty of God.

SWANAGE, DORSET, J. B. PHILLIPS
1956

THE BOOK OF REVELATION

AUTHOR: *John the Apostle, John the Elder or another leading Christian by the name of John.*

(Justin Martyr in his "Dialogue with Trypho the Jew", written about 140, appears to ascribe the authorship of this book to John the Apostle. But Dionysius, Bishop of Alexandria from 249 to 265, a learned and holy man, could not accept John the Apostle as the author of this Revelation, and gave almost conclusive reasons for his opinion. Since those early days there has been much argument, and much research has gone into the problem of establishing authorship but without conclusive result. It is essential that the reader should study a good commentary on the subject of authorship, so that he may appreciate the difficulties involved. *Some books are listed on page 21.)*

DATE: *Probably about 95, but some hold to an earlier date.*

DESTINATION: *This book is plainly intended primarily for the Seven Churches of Asia. But since the Message of the book is relevant to all Christians under persecution, and since the book treats of Divine Judgments upon the whole world, the author must surely have intended it to be circulated among all Christian communities.*

THEME: *This book consists of a series of visions granted to John while in exile for his Christian witness. The language is highly symbolic and figurative, and attempts in modern days to fit its prophecies into contemporary situations have led interpreters into all kinds of difficulties. It is thought by many that the symbols and figures of the book would be understood by the Christians to whom the book was first sent, but that the key to their interpretation has now been lost. However, certain themes emerge distinctly for the modern reader's profit:*

(1) *The absolute sovereignty of God, and His ultimate purpose to destroy all forms of evil.*

(2) *The inevitable judgments of God upon evil, upon the worship of false gods, which include riches, power and success.*

(3) *The necessity for patient endurance, the ultimate security being the knowledge that God is in control of history.*

(4) *The existence of reality, represented here under such symbols as the New Jerusalem, apart and secure from the battles and tribulations of earthly life, promises complete spiritual security to those who are faithful to God and His Christ.*

(5) *The glimpses of worship and adoration, constantly offered to God and the Lamb, are a kind of pattern of man's ultimate acknowledgment of the Character of God when he sees Him as He is.*

But for any proper appreciation of the themes of this mysterious book it is imperative that the reader should make use of one or more commentaries.

SPECIAL NOTE: *The Greek of this book is peculiar in construction and is occasionally ungrammatical. Sometimes, in the visions for instance, there is a mixing of past and present tenses. After careful consideration the translator has decided not to reproduce these oddities, except where a sudden change of tense adds vividness to the description.*

SUGGESTED BOOKS FOR FURTHER STUDY

Commentaries on The Book of Revelation:

The Moffatt New Testament Commentary: Martin Kiddle (Hodder & Stoughton)

A Rebirth of Images: Austin Farrer (Dacre Press)

The Torch Bible Commentaries: Preston and Hanson (S.C.M. Press)

The Cambridge Bible: Simcox (C.U.P.)

The Century Bible: Anderson Scott (T. C. & E. C. Jack)

and the relevant sections in the following:

Peake's Commentary on the Bible (Nelson)

Concise Bible Commentary: Lowther Clarke (S.P.C.K.)

The Teacher's Commentary (S.C.M. Press)

The I.V.F. Commentary (Tyndale Press)

Introducing the New Testament: A. M. Hunter (S.C.M. Press)

An Introduction to the New Testament: W. G. Robinson (Edward Arnold Co.)

THE REVELATION OF JOHN

Concerning this book 1:1

This is a Revelation from Jesus Christ, which God gave Him so that He might show His servants what must very soon take place. He made it known by sending His angel to His servant John, who is the witness of all that he saw—the Message of God, and the Testimony of Jesus Christ.

Happy is the man who reads this prophecy and happy are those who hear it read and pay attention to its Message; for the time is near.

John's greeting and ascription 1:4

John, to the Seven Churches in Asia:

Grace and peace be to you from Him Who is and Who was and Who is coming, from the Seven Spirits before His Throne, and from Jesus Christ the faithful Witness, First-born of the dead, and Ruler of kings upon earth. To Him Who loves us and has set us free from our sins through His own blood, Who has made us a kingdom of priests to His God and Father, to Him be glory and power for timeless ages, Amen!

See, He is coming in the clouds and every eye

shall see Him, even those Who pierced Him, and His coming will mean bitter sorrow to every tribe upon the earth. So let it be!

"I am Alpha and Omega," says the Lord God, "Who is and Who was and Who is coming, the Almighty."

The Message to the Seven Churches 1:9

I, John, who am your brother and your companion in the distress, the kingdom and the faithful endurance to which Jesus calls us, was on the island called Patmos because I had spoken God's Message and borne witness to Jesus. On the Lord's Day I knew myself inspired by the Spirit, and I heard from behind me a voice loud as a trumpet-call, saying,

"Write down in a book what you see, and send it to the Seven Churches—to Ephesus, Smyrna, Pergamum, Thyatira, Sardis, Philadelphia and Laodicea!"

I turned to see whose voice it was that was speaking to me, and when I had turned I saw seven golden lampstands, and among these lampstands I saw someone like a Son of Man. He was dressed in a long robe with a golden girdle around His breast; His head and His hair were white as snow-white wool, His eyes blazed like fire, and His feet shone as the finest bronze glows in the furnace. His voice had the sound of a great waterfall, and I saw that in His right hand He held seven stars. A sharp two-edged sword came out of His mouth, and His face was ablaze like the sun at its height.

When my eyes took in this sight I fell at His feet like a dead man. And then He placed His right hand upon me and said,

"Do not be afraid. I am the First and the Last, the Living One. I am He Who was dead, and now you see Me alive for timeless ages! I hold in My hand the keys of Death and the Grave. Therefore, write down what you have seen, both the things which are now, and the things which are to be hereafter. The secret meaning of the seven stars which you saw in My right hand, and of the seven golden lampstands is this: the seven stars are the angels of the seven Churches and the seven lampstands are the Churches themselves."

1. *To the Loveless Church* 2:1

"Write this to the angel of the Church in Ephesus: These words are spoken by the One Who holds the seven stars safe in His right hand, and Who walks among the seven golden lampstands. I know what you have done; I know how hard you have worked and what you have endured. I know that you will not tolerate wicked men, that you have put to the test self-styled 'Apostles', who are nothing of the sort, and have found them to be liars. I know your powers of endurance—how you have suffered for the sake of My Name and have not grown weary. But I hold this against you, that you do not love as you did at first. Remember then how far you have fallen. Repent and live as you lived at first. Otherwise, if your heart remains unchanged, I shall come to you and remove your lampstand from its place.

2:6

Yet you have this to your credit, that you hate the practices of the Nicolaitans, which I Myself detest. Let every listener hear what the Spirit says to the Churches:

To the victorious I will give the right to eat from the Tree of Life which grows in the Paradise of God.

2. *To the Persecuted Church* 2:8

"Write this to the angel of the Church in Smyrna:

These words are spoken by the First and the Last, Who died and came to life again. I know of your tribulation and of your poverty—though in fact you are rich! I know how you are slandered by those who call themselves Jews, but in fact are no Jews but a synagogue of Satan. Have no fear of what you will suffer. I tell you now that the Devil is going to cast some of your number into prison where your faith will be tested and your distress will last for ten days. Be faithful in the face of death and I will give you the crown of life. Let every listener hear what the Spirit says to the Churches:

The victorious cannot suffer the slightest hurt from the Second Death.

3. *To the Over-tolerant Church* 2:12

"Write this to the angel of the Church in Pergamum:

These words are spoken by Him Who has the sharp two-edged sword. I know where you live—where Satan sits enthroned. I know that you hold fast to My Name and that you never denied your faith in Me even in the days when Antipas, My faithful witness, was martyred before your eyes in the very house of Satan.

Yet I have a few things against you—some of your number cling to the teaching of Balaam, the man who taught Balak how to entice the children of Israel into eating meat sacrificed to idols and into sexual immorality. I have also against you the fact that among your number are some who hold just as closely to the teaching of the Nicolaitans. Repent then, or else I shall come to you quickly and make war upon them with the sword of My mouth. Let the listener hear what the Spirit says to the Churches:

I will give the victorious some of the hidden manna, and I will also give him a white stone with a new name written upon it which no man knows except the man who receives it.

4. *To the Compromising Church* 2:18

"Write this to the angel of the Church in Thyatira:

These are the words of the Son of God Whose eyes blaze like fire and Whose feet shine like the finest bronze:

I know what you have done. I know of your love and your loyalty, your service and your endurance. Moreover, I know that you are doing more than you did at first. But I have this against you, that you tolerate that woman Jezebel who calls herself a prophetess, but who by her teaching deceives my servants into sexual immorality and eating idols'-meat. I have given her time to repent but she has shown no desire to repent of her immorality. See, now, how I throw her into bed and her lovers with her, and I will send them terrible suffering unless they repent of what she has done. As for her children, I shall strike them dead. Then all the Churches will know that I am the One Who searches men's hearts and minds, and that I will reward each one of you according to your deeds.

But for the rest of you at Thyatira, who do not hold this teaching, and have not learned what they call 'the deep things of Satan', I will lay no further burden upon you, except that you hold on to what you have until I come!

To the one who is victorious, who carries out My work to the end, I will give authority over the nations, just as I Myself have received authority from My Father, and I will give him the morning star. He shall 'shepherd them with a rod of iron'; he shall 'dash them in pieces like a potter's vessel'. Let the listener hear what the Spirit says to the Churches.

5. *To the Sleeping Church* 3:1

"Write this to the angel of the Church in Sardis:

These are the words of Him Who holds in His hand the seven Spirits of God and the seven stars:

I know what you have done, that you have a reputation for being alive, but that in fact you are dead. Now wake up! Strengthen what you still have before it dies! For I have not found any of your deeds complete in the sight of My God. Remember then what you were given and what you were taught. Hold to those things and repent. If you refuse to wake up, then I will come to you like a thief, and you will have no idea of the hour of My coming.

Yet you still have a few names in Sardis of people who have not soiled their garments. They shall walk with Me in white, for they have deserved to do so. The victorious shall wear such white garments, and never will I erase his name from the Book of Life. Indeed, I will speak his name openly in the presence of My Father and of His angels. Let the listener hear what the Spirit says to the Churches.

6. *To the Church with opportunity* 3:7

"Then write this to the angel of the Church in Philadelphia:

These are the words of the Holy One and the True, Who holds the key of David, Who opens and no man shall shut, and Who shuts and no man shall open. I know what you have done. See, I have given you a door flung wide open, which no man can close! For you have some little power and have been faithful to My Message and have not denied My Name. See how I deal with those of Satan's synagogue, who claim to be Jews, yet are no Jews but liars! Watch how I make them come and bow down before your feet and acknowledge that I have loved you. Because you have obeyed My call to patient endurance I will keep you safe from the hour of trial which is to come upon the whole world, to test all who live upon the earth. I am coming soon; hold fast to what you have—let no one deprive you of your crown. As for the victorious, I will make him a pillar in the Temple of My God, and he will never leave it. I will write upon him the Name of My God, and the name of the City of My God, the New Jerusalem which comes down out of Heaven from My God. And I will write upon him My own new Name. Let the listener hear what the Spirit says to the Churches.

7. *To the Complacent Church* 3:14

"Then write this to the angel of the Church in Laodicea:

These are the words of the Amen, the faithful and true Witness, the Beginning of God's Creation:

I know what you have done, and that you are neither cold nor hot. I could wish that you were either cold or hot! But since you are lukewarm and neither hot nor cold, I intend to spit you out of my mouth! While you say, 'I am rich, I have prospered, and there is nothing that I need', you have no eyes to see that you are wretched, pitiable, poverty-stricken, blind and naked. My advice to you is to buy from Me that gold which is purified in the furnace so that you may be rich, and white garments to wear so that you may hide the shame of your nakedness, and salve to put on your eyes to make you see. All those whom I love I correct and discipline. Therefore, shake off your complacency and repent. See, I stand knocking at the door. If anyone listens to My Voice and opens the door, I will go into his house and dine with him, and he with Me. As for the victorious, I will give him the honour of sitting beside Me on My Throne, just as I Myself have won the victory and have taken My seat beside My Father on His Throne. Let the listener hear what the Spirit says to the Churches."

The vision of Heaven 4:1

Later I looked again, and before my eyes a door stood open in Heaven, and in my ears was the voice with the ring of a trumpet, which I had heard at first, speaking to me and saying,

"Come up here, and I will show you what must happen in the future."

Immediately I knew myself to be inspired by the Spirit, and in my vision I saw that a Throne had been set up in Heaven, and there was someone seated upon the Throne. His appearance blazed like diamond and topaz, and all around the Throne shone a halo like an emerald rainbow. In a circle around the Throne there were twenty-four thrones and seated upon them twenty-four Elders dressed in white with golden crowns upon their heads. From the central Throne come flashes of lightning, noises and peals of thunder. Seven lamps are burning before the Throne, and they are the seven Spirits of God. In front of the Throne there appears a sea of glass as clear as crystal. On each side, encircling the Throne, are four Living Creatures covered with eyes in front and behind. The first Living Creature is like a lion, the second is like a calf, the third has a face like a man, and the fourth Living Creature appears like an eagle in flight. These four Creatures have each of them six wings and are covered with eyes, all around them, and even within them. Day and night they never cease to say,

"Holy, holy, holy is the Lord God, the Almighty, Who was and Who is and Who is coming."

The ceaseless worship of Heaven 4:9

And whenever the Living Creatures give glory and honour and thanksgiving to the One Who sits upon the Throne, Who lives for timeless ages, the twenty-four Elders prostrate themselves before Him Who is seated upon the Throne and worship the One Who lives for timeless ages. They cast their crowns before the Throne and say,

"Thou art worthy, O Lord our God, to receive glory and honour and power, for Thou didst create all things; by Thy Will they existed and were created."

The sealed book of future events 5:1

Then I noticed in the right hand of the One seated upon the Throne a book filled with writing both inside and on its back, and it was sealed with seven seals. And I saw a mighty angel who called out in a loud voice,

"Who is fit to open the book and break its seals?"

And no one in Heaven or upon earth or under the earth was able to open the book, or even to look at it. I began to weep bitterly because no one could be found fit to open the book, or even to look at it, when one of the Elders said to me,

"Do not weep. See, the Lion from the tribe of Judah, the Root of David, has won the victory and is able to open the book and break its seven seals."

Then, standing in the very centre of the Throne and of the four Living Creatures and of the Elders, I saw a Lamb that seemed to have been slaughtered. He had seven horns and seven eyes, which are the seven Spirits of God and are sent out into every corner of the earth. Then He came and took the book from the right hand of Him Who was seated upon the Throne.

The new hymn of the created and of the redeemed 5:8

When He had taken the book, the four Living Creatures and the twenty-four Elders prostrated themselves before the Lamb. Each of them had a harp, and they had golden bowls full of incense, which are the prayers of the saints. They sang a new song and these are the words they sang:

"Worthy art Thou to take the book and break its seals, for Thou has been slain and by Thy blood hast purchased for God men from every tribe, and tongue, and people, and nation! Thou has made them a kingdom of priests for our God, and they shall reign as kings upon the earth."

The hymn of the whole company of Heaven 5:11

Then in my vision I heard the voices of many angels encircling the Throne, the Living Creatures and the Elders. There were myriads of myriads and thousands of thousands, crying in a great voice,

"Worthy is the Lamb Who was slain, to receive power and riches and wisdom, and strength and honour and glory and blessing!"

Then I heard the voice of everything created in Heaven, upon earth, under the earth and upon the sea, and all that are in them saying,

"Blessing and Honour and Glory and Power be given to Him Who sits upon the Throne, and to the Lamb, for timeless ages!"

The four Living Creatures said, "Amen", while the Elders fell down and worshipped.

THE LAMB BREAKS THE SEALS

The first rider: conquest 6:1

Then I watched while the Lamb broke one of the seven seals, and I heard one of the four Living Creatures say in a voice of thunder,

"Come out!"

I looked, and before my eyes was a white horse.

Its rider carried a bow, and he was given a crown. He rode out conquering and bent on conquest.

The second rider: war 6:3

Then, when the Lamb broke the second seal, I heard the second Living Creature cry,

"Come out!"

And another horse came forth, red in colour. Its rider was given power to deprive the earth of peace, so that men should kill each other. A huge sword was put into his hand.

The third rider: famine 6:5

When the Lamb broke the third seal, I heard the third Living Creature say,

"Come out!"

I looked again and there before my eyes was a black horse. Its rider had a pair of scales in his hand, and I heard a voice which seemed to come from the four Living Creatures, saying,

"A quart of wheat for a shilling, and three quarts of barley for a shilling—but no tampering with the oil or the wine!"

The fourth rider: death 6:7

Then, when He broke the fourth seal I heard the voice of the fourth Living Creature cry,

"Come out!"

Again I looked, and there appeared a horse sickly green in colour. The name of its rider was Death, and the Grave followed close behind him. A quarter of the earth was put into their power, to kill with the sword, by famine, by violence, and through the wild beasts of the earth.

The cry of the martyrs in Heaven 6:9

When the Lamb broke the fifth seal, I could see, beneath the Altar, the souls of those who had been killed for the sake of the Word of God and because of the faithfulness of their witness. They cried out in a loud voice, saying.

"How long shall it be, O Lord of All, holy and true, before Thou shalt judge and avenge our blood upon the inhabitants of the earth?"

Then each of them was given a white robe, and they were told to be patient a little longer, until the number of their fellow-servants and of their brethren, who were to die as they had died, should be complete.

The awe-full wrath of God 6:12

Then I watched while He broke the sixth seal. There was a tremendous earthquake, the sun turned dark like coarse black cloth, and the full moon was red as blood. The stars of the sky fell upon the earth, just as a fig-tree sheds unripe figs when shaken in a gale. The sky vanished as though it were a scroll being rolled up, and every mountain and island was jolted out of its place. Then the kings of the earth, and the great men, the captains, the wealthy, the powerful, and every man, whether slave or free, hid themselves in caves and among mountain rocks. They called out to the mountains and the rocks,

"Fall down upon us and hide us from the Face of Him Who sits upon the Throne, and from the wrath of the Lamb! For the great day of their wrath has come, and who can stand against it?"

Judgment stayed for the sealing of God's people 7:1

Later I saw four angels standing at the four corners of the earth holding in check the four winds of the earth that none should blow upon the earth or upon the sea or upon any tree. Then I saw another angel ascending out of the east, holding the seal of the living God. He cried out in a loud voice to the four angels who had the power to harm the earth and the sea:

"Do no harm to the earth, nor to the sea, nor to the trees until we have sealed the servants of our God upon their foreheads."

I heard the number of those who were thus sealed and it was 144,000, from every tribe of the sons of Israel. Twelve thousand were sealed from the tribe of Judah; twelve thousand from the tribe of Reuben; twelve thousand from the tribe of Gad; twelve thousand from the tribe of Asher; twelve thousand from the tribe of Naphtali; twelve thousand from the tribe of Manasseh; twelve thousand from the tribe of Simeon; twelve thousand from the tribe of Levi; twelve thousand from the tribe of Issachar; twelve thousand from the tribe of Zebulun; twelve thousand from the tribe of Joseph; and twelve thousand were sealed from the tribe of Benjamin.

The countless host of the redeemed 7:9

When this was done I looked again, and before my eyes appeared a vast crowd beyond man's power to number. They came from every nation and tribe and people and language, and they stood before the Throne of the Lamb, dressed in white robes with palm-branches in their hands. With a great voice they shouted these words:

"Salvation belongs to our God Who sits upon the Throne and to the Lamb!"

Then all the angels stood encircling the Throne, the Elders and the four Living Creatures, and prostrated themselves with heads bowed before the Throne and worshipped God, saying,

"Amen! Blessing and Glory and Wisdom and Thanksgiving and Honour and Power and Strength be given to our God for timeless ages!"

The countless host explained 7:13

Then one of the Elders addressed me and asked,

"These who are dressed in white robes—who are they, and where do they come from?"

"You know, my Lord," I answered him.

Then he told me,

"These are those who have come through the Great Oppression; they have washed their robes and made them white in the blood of the Lamb. That is why they now have their place before the Throne of God, and serve Him day and night in His Temple. He Who sits upon the Throne will be their Shelter. They will never again know hunger or thirst. The sun shall never beat upon them, neither shall there be any scorching heat, for the Lamb Who is in the centre of the Throne will be their Shepherd and will lead them to springs of Living Water. And God will wipe away every tear from their eyes."

The seventh seal: complete silence 8:1

Then, when He had broken the seventh seal, there was utter silence in Heaven for what seemed to me half-an-hour.

The vision of the seven trumpeters 8:2

Then I saw the seven angels who stand in the presence of God, and seven trumpets were put into their hands.

Then another angel came and stood by the Altar holding a golden censer. He was given a great quantity of incense to add to the prayers of all the saints, to be laid upon the golden Altar before the Throne. And the smoke of the incense rose up before God from the angel's hand, mingled with the prayers of the saints. Then the angel took the censer, filled it with fire from the Altar, and hurled it upon the earth. And at that there were thunderings and noises, flashes of lightning and an earthquake.

Then the seven angels who were holding the seven trumpets prepared to blow them.

The first trumpet: hail and fire 8:7

The first angel blew his trumpet. Hail and fire mingled with blood appeared, and were hurled upon the earth. One-third of the earth was burnt up, one-third of all the trees was burnt up, and every blade of green grass was burnt up.

The second trumpet: the blazing mountain 8:8

The second angel blew his trumpet, and something like a vast mountain blazing with fire was thrown into the sea. A third-part of the sea turned into blood, a third of all live creatures in the sea died, and a third-part of all shipping was destroyed.

The third trumpet: the poisonous star 8:10

Then the third angel blew his trumpet and there fell from the sky a huge star blazing like a torch. It fell upon a third of the rivers and springs of water. The name of the star is said to be Apsinthus (Wormwood). A third of all the waters turned into wormwood, and many people died because the waters had become so bitter.

The fourth trumpet: light from the sky diminishes 8:12

The fourth angel blew his trumpet, and a third-part of the sun, a third-part of the moon and a third of the stars were struck. A third-part of the light of each of them was darkened, so that light by day and light by night were both diminished by a third-part.

The cry of pity from mid-heaven 8:13

Then in my vision I saw a solitary eagle* flying in mid-heaven, crying in a loud voice,

"Alas, alas, alas for the inhabitants of the earth for there are three more trumpet blasts which the three angels shall sound!"

The fifth trumpet: the fathomless pit 9:1

The fifth angel blew his trumpet. I saw a star that had fallen down from Heaven to earth, and he was given the key to the fathomless Pit. Then he opened the Pit and smoke like the smoke of a vast furnace rose out of it, so that the light of the sun and the air itself grew dark from the smoke of the Pit.

* Not "angel", as in A.V.

Then out of the smoke emerged locusts to descend upon the earth. They were given powers like those of earthly scorpions. They had orders to do no harm to any grass, green thing or tree upon the earth, but to injure only those human beings who did not bear the seal of God upon their foreheads. They were given no power to kill men, but only to torture them for five months. The torture they could inflict was like the pain of a scorpion's sting.

In those days men will seek death but they will never find it; they will long to die but death will elude them. These locusts looked to me in my vision like horses prepared for battle. On their heads were what appeared to be crowns like gold; their faces were like human faces, and they had long hair like women. Their teeth were like lions' teeth, their breasts were like iron-breastplates, and the noise of their wings was like the noise of a host of chariots and horses charging into battle. They have tails and stings like scorpions, and it is in their tails that they possess the power to injure men for five months. They have as their king the angel of the Pit, whose name in Hebrew is Abaddon and in Greek Apollyon, (meaning the Destroyer).

The first Disaster is now past, but I see two more approaching.

The sixth trumpet: the destroying Angels 9:13

Then the sixth angel blew his trumpet, and I heard a solitary voice speaking from the four corners of the golden Altar that stands in the presence of God. And it said to the sixth angel who held the trumpet,

"Release the four angels who are bound at the great river Euphrates!"

Then these four angels who had been held ready for the hour, the day, the month and the year, were set free to kill a third-part of all mankind. The number of their horsemen was two hundred million—I heard what their number was. In my vision I saw these horses and their riders, and their breastplates were fiery-red, blue and yellow. The horses' heads looked to me like the heads of lions, and out of their mouths poured fire and smoke and sulphur. A third of all mankind died from the fearful effects of these three, the fire, the smoke and the sulphur which pours out of their mouths. For the power of these horses lies in their mouths and in their tails. Indeed their tails are like serpents with heads, and with these they inflict injury.

The rest of mankind, who did not die in this fearful destruction, neither repented of the works of their own hands nor ceased to worship evil powers and idols of gold, silver, brass, stone or wood, which can neither see nor hear nor move. Neither did they repent of their murders, their sorceries, their sexual sins, nor of their thieving.

The Angel with the little book 10:1

Then I saw another mighty angel descending from Heaven. He was clothed in a cloud, and there was a rainbow around his head. His face blazed like the sun, his legs like pillars of fire, and he had a little book lying open in his hand. He planted his right foot on the sea and his left foot on the land, and then shouted with a loud voice like the roar of a lion. And when he shouted the seven thunders lifted their voices. When the seven thunders had rolled I was on the point of writing but I heard a voice from Heaven, saying,

"Seal up what the seven thunders said, but do not write it down!"

Then the angel whom I had seen bestriding the sea and the land raised his right hand to Heaven and swore by the Living One of the timeless ages, Who created Heaven, earth and sea and all that is in them:

"There shall be no more delay! In the days which shall soon be announced by the trumpet-blast of the seventh angel the Mysterious Purpose of God shall be completed, as He assured His servants the prophets."

Then the voice which I had heard from Heaven was again in my ears, saying,

"Go and take the little book which lies open in the hand of the angel whose feet are planted on both sea and land."

So I went off towards the angel, asking him to give me the little book.

"Take it," he said to me, "and eat it up. It will be bitter to your stomach, but sweet as honey in your mouth."

Then I took the little book from the angel's hand and swallowed it. It was as sweet as honey to the taste but when I had eaten it up it was bitter to my stomach.

John is instructed to prophesy 10:11

Then they said to me, "It is again your duty to prophesy about many peoples, nations, languages and kings." And I was given a measuring rod like a staff, and I was told, "Get up and measure the Temple of God, and the Altar, and count those who worship there. But leave out of your measurement the courtyard outside the Temple—do not measure that at all. For it has been given over to the nations, and they will trample over the Holy City for forty-two months."

God's two witnesses 11:3

"And I will give authority to my Two Witnesses to proclaim the Message, clothed in sackcloth for twelve hundred and sixty days."

These are the two olive trees and the two lampstands which stand before the Lord of the earth.

If anyone tries to harm them, fire issues from their mouths and consumes their enemies. Indeed, if anyone should try to hurt them, this is the way in which he will certainly meet his death. These Witnesses have power to shut up the sky and stop any rain from falling during the time of their preaching. Moreover, they have power to turn the waters into blood, and to strike the earth with any plague as often as they wish.

The emergence of the animal 11:7

Then, when their work of witness is complete, the Animal will come up out of the Pit and go to war with them. It will conquer and kill them, and their bodies will lie in the street of the great City, which is called by those with spiritual understanding, "Sodom" and "Egypt"—the very place where their Lord Himself was crucified. For three and a half days men from all peoples and tribes and languages and nations will gaze upon their bodies and will not allow them to be buried. The inhabitants of the earth will gloat over them and will hold celebrations and send one another presents, because these two prophets had brought such misery to the inhabitants of the earth.

The resurrection and ascension of the two witnesses 11:11

But after three and a half days the Spirit of Life from God entered them and they stood upright on their feet. This struck terror into the hearts of those who were watching them, and they heard a tremendous Voice speaking to these two from Heaven, saying,

"Come up here!"

And they went up to Heaven in a cloud in full view of their enemies. And at that moment there was a great earthquake, a tenth-part of the City fell in ruins and seven thousand people were known to have been killed in the earthquake. The rest were terrified and acknowledged the glory of the God of Heaven.

The seventh trumpet: (i) the worship of Heaven 11:14

The second Disaster is now past, and I see the third Disaster following hard upon the heels of the second. The seventh angel blew his trumpet. There arose loud voices in Heaven and they were saying,

"The Kingship of the World now belongs to our Lord and to His Christ, and He shall be King for timeless ages!"

Then the twenty-four Elders, who sit upon their thrones in the presence of God, prostrated themselves and, with bowed heads, worshipped God, saying:

"We thank Thee, O Lord Who art God the Almighty, Who art and Who wast, that Thou hast assumed Thy great power and hast become King. The nations were full of fury, but now Thy wrath has come and with it the time for the dead to be judged and for reward to be given to Thy servants, the prophets and the saints, and all who fear Thy Name, both small and great. Now is the time for destroying the destroyers of the earth!"

Then the Temple of God in Heaven was thrown open and the Ark of His Agreement within His Temple could be clearly seen. Accompanying this sight were flashes of lightning, loud noises, peals of thunder, an earthquake and a violent storm of hail.

The seventh trumpet: (ii) the sign of the woman 12:1

Then a huge sign became visible in the sky—the figure of a Woman clothed with the sun, with the moon under her feet and a crown of twelve stars upon her head. She was pregnant, and cried out in her labour and in the pains of bringing forth her child.

The seventh trumpet: (iii) the dragon, the enemy of the woman 12:3

Then another sign became visible in the sky, and I saw that it was a huge red Dragon with seven heads and ten horns, with a diadem upon each of his heads. His tail swept down a third of the stars in the sky and hurled them upon the earth. The Dragon took his place in front of the Woman who was about to give birth to a child, so that as soon as she did so he might devour it. She gave birth to a male child who is to shepherd all the nations "with a rod of iron". Her child was snatched up to God and to His Throne, while the Woman fled into the desert where she has a place prepared for her by God's command. There they will take care of her for twelve hundred and sixty days.

War in Heaven 12:7

Then war broke out in Heaven. Michael and his angels battled with the Dragon. The Dragon and his angels fought back, but they did not prevail and they were expelled from Heaven. So the huge Dragon, the Serpent of ancient times, who is called the Devil and Satan, the Deceiver of the whole world, was hurled down upon the earth, and his angels were hurled down with him.

The victory of Heaven proclaimed 12:10

Then I heard a great voice in Heaven cry:

"Now the Salvation and the Power and Kingdom of our God, and the Authority of His Christ have come! For the Accuser of our brethren has been thrown down from his place, where he stood before our God accusing them day and night. Now they have conquered him through the blood of the Lamb, and through the Word to which they bore witness. They did not cherish life even in the face of death!

"Therefore, rejoice, O Heavens, and all you who live in the Heavens! But alas for the earth and the sea, for the Devil has come down to you in great fury, knowing that his time is short!"

The dragon's enmity against the woman 12:13

And when the Dragon saw that he had been cast down upon the earth, he began to pursue the Woman who had given birth to the male child. But she was given two great eagle's wings so that she could fly to her place in the desert, where she is kept safe from the Serpent for a time and times and half a time. Then the Serpent ejected water from his mouth, streaming like a river in pursuit of the Woman, to drown her in its flood. But the earth came to the Woman's rescue, opened its mouth and swallowed up the river which the Dragon had emitted from his mouth. Then the Dragon raged with fury against the Woman and went off to make war against the rest of her children—those who keep the commandments of God and bear their witness to Jesus.

The animal from the sea 13:1

Then, as I stood on the sand of the sea-shore, there rose out of the sea before my eyes an Animal with seven heads and ten horns. There were diadems upon its horns and blasphemous names upon its heads. The Animal which I saw had the appearance of a leopard, though it had the feet of a bear and a mouth like the mouth of a lion. Then the Dragon gave it his own power and throne and great authority. One of its heads appeared to have been wounded to death but the mortal wound had healed.

The whole earth followed the Animal with wonder, and they worshipped the Dragon because he had given authority to the Animal. Then they worshipped the Animal, too, saying,

"Who is like the Animal? Who could make war against it?"

It was allowed to speak monstrous blasphemies and to exert its authority for forty-two months.

So it poured out blasphemies against God, blaspheming His Name and His Dwelling-place and those who live in Heaven. Moreover, it was permitted to make war upon the saints and to conquer them; the authority given to it extended over every tribe and people and language and nation. All the inhabitants of the earth will worship it—all those whose names have not been written in the Book of Life which belongs to the Lamb slain from the foundation of the world.

Parenthetical: a word to the reader 13:9

Let the listener hear this:

If any man is destined for captivity he will go into captivity. If any man kills with the sword he must himself be killed with the sword. Amid all this stands the endurance and faith of the saints.

The animal from the earth 13:11

Then I saw another Animal rising out of the earth, and it had two horns like a lamb but it spoke in the voice of a dragon. It uses the full authority of the first Animal in its presence. It compels the earth and all its inhabitants to worship the first Animal—the one with the mortal wound which had healed. It performs great signs: before men's eyes it makes fire fall down from heaven to earth. It deceives the inhabitants of the earth by the signs which it is allowed to perform in the presence of the Animal, and it tells them to make a statue in honour of the Animal which received the sword-thrust and yet survived. Further, it was allowed to give the breath of life to the statue of the Animal so that the statue could speak and condemn to death all those who do not worship its statue. Then it compels all, small and great, rich and poor, free men and slaves, to receive a mark on their right hands or on their foreheads. The purpose of this is that no one should be able to buy or sell unless he bears the mark of the name of the Animal or the number of its name. Understanding is needed here: let every thinking man calculate the number of the Animal. It is the number of a man, and its number is six hundred and sixty-six.*

The vision of the lamb and the first of the redeemed 14:1

Then I looked again and before my eyes the Lamb was standing on Mount Sion, and with Him were a hundred and forty-four thousand who had His Name and His Father's Name written upon their foreheads. Then I heard a sound coming from Heaven like the roar of a great waterfall and the heavy rolling of thunder. Yet the sound which I heard was also like the music of harpists sweeping their strings. And now they are singing a new song of praise before the Throne, and before the four Living Creatures and the Elders.

* This number undoubtedly refers to NERO ÇAESAR, by means of a simple Hebrew cipher. Guesses about its later application have been rife throughout the centuries. The triple six stands for a concentration of evil, six being the number of imperfection.

No one could learn that song except the one hundred and forty-four thousand who had been redeemed from the earth. These are the men who have never defiled themselves with women, for they are celibate. These are the men who follow the Lamb wherever He may go; these men have been redeemed from among mankind as first-fruits to God and to the Lamb. They have never been guilty of any falsehood; they are beyond reproach.

The Angel with the gospel 14:6

Then I saw another angel flying in mid-heaven, holding the everlasting Gospel to proclaim to the inhabitants of the earth—to every nation and tribe and language and people. He was crying in a loud voice,

"Reverence God, and give glory to Him; for the hour of His Judgment has come! Worship Him Who made Heaven and earth, the sea and the springs of water."

The Angel of doom 14:8

Then another, a second angel, followed him crying,

"Fallen, fallen is Babylon the Great! She who made all nations drink the wine of her passionate unfaithfulness!"

The Angel of judgment 14:9

Then a third angel followed these two, crying in a loud voice,

"If any man worships the Animal and its statue and bears its mark upon his forehead or upon his hand, then that man shall drink the wine of God's passion, poured undiluted into the cup of His Wrath. He shall be tortured by fire and sulphur in the presence of the Holy angels and of the Lamb. The smoke of such men's torture ascends for timeless ages, and there is no respite from it day or night. Such are the worshippers of the Animal and its statue, and among their number are all who bear the mark of its name."

The call to stand fast 14:12

In all this stands the endurance of the saints—those who keep the commandments of God and their faith in Jesus.

The security of the saints 14:13

Then I heard a voice from Heaven, saying,

"Write this! From henceforth happy are the dead who die in the Lord!"

"Happy indeed," says the Spirit, "for they rest from their labours and their deeds go with them!"

The harvest of God's wrath 14:14

Once again I looked, and a white cloud appeared before me with someone sitting upon the cloud with the appearance of a Man. He had a golden crown on his head, and held a sharp sickle in his hand. Then another angel came out from the Temple, calling in a loud voice to the one sitting on the cloud,

"Thrust in your sickle and reap, for the time of reaping has come and the harvest of the earth is fully ripe!"

Then the one sitting upon the cloud swung his sickle upon the earth, and the reaping of the earth was done.

Then another angel came out from the Temple in Heaven, and he also had a sharp sickle. Yet another angel came out from the Altar where he has command over the fire, and called out in a loud voice to the angel with the sharp sickle,

"Thrust in your sharp sickle and harvest the clusters from the vineyard of the earth for the grapes are fully ripe!"

Then the angel swung his sickle upon the earth and gathered the harvest of the earth's vineyard, and threw it into the great winepress of the Wrath of God. The grapes were trodden outside the City, and out of the winepress flowed blood for two hundred miles in a stream as high as the horses' bridles.

The seven last plagues prepared 15:1

Then I saw another Sign in Heaven, vast and awe-inspiring: seven angels are holding the seven last plagues, and with these the Wrath of God is brought to an end.

The hymn of the redeemed 15:2

And I saw what appeared to be a sea of glass shot through with fire, and upon this glassy sea were standing those who had emerged victorious from the fight with the Animal, its statue and the number which denotes its name. In their hands they hold harps which God has given them, and they are singing the song of Moses the servant of God, and the song of the Lamb, and these are the words they sing:

"Great and wonderful are Thy works, O Lord God, the Almighty! Just and true are Thy ways, Thou King of the nations! Who should not reverence Thee, O Lord, and glorify Thy Name? For Thou alone art holy; therefore all nations shall come and worship before Thee, for Thy just judgments have been made plain!"

The Angels leave the temple of God— 15:5

Later in my vision I saw the Temple of the Tabernacle of Testimony in Heaven wide open, and out of the Temple came forth the seven angels who hold the seven plagues. They were dressed in spotless shining linen, and they were girded round their breasts with golden girdles.

Then one of the four Living Creatures gave to the seven angels seven golden bowls filled with the Wrath of God Who lives for timeless ages. The Temple was filled with smoke from the glory and power of God, and no one could enter the Temple until the seven plagues of the seven angels were past and over.

—and are ordered to pour out the bowls of His wrath 16:1

Then I heard a loud voice from the Temple saying to the seven angels,

"Go and pour out upon the earth the seven bowls of the Wrath of God!"

The first bowl: ulcers 16:2

The first angel went off and emptied his bowl upon the earth. Whereupon loathsome and malignant ulcers attacked all those who bore the mark of the Animal and worshipped its statue.

The second bowl: death in the sea 16:3

The second angel emptied his bowl into the sea, which turned into a fluid like the blood of a corpse, and every living thing in it died.

The third bowl: water becomes blood 16:4

Then the third angel emptied his bowl into the rivers and springs of water, and they turned into blood. And I heard the angel of the waters say,

"Just art Thou in these Thy judgments, Thou Who art and wast the holy One! For they have spilled the blood of saints and prophets, and now Thou hast given them blood to drink. They have what they deserve."

And I heard the Altar say,

"Yes, O Lord, God Almighty, Thy judgments are true and right."

The fourth bowl: scorching heat 16:8

The fourth angel emptied his bowl over the sun, and the sun was given power to scorch men in its fiery blaze. Then men were terribly burned in the heat, and they blasphemed the Name of God Who has control over these afflictions; but they neither repented nor gave Him glory.

The fifth bowl: the plague of darkness 16:10

Then the fifth angel emptied his bowl upon the throne of the Animal. Its kingdom was plunged into darkness; men gnawed their tongues in agony, cursed the God of Heaven for their pain and their ulcers, but refused to repent of what they had done.

The sixth bowl: the great river dried up 16:12

Then the sixth angel emptied his bowl upon the great river Euphrates. The waters of that river were dried up to prepare a road for the kings from the East. And then I noticed three foul spirits, looking like frogs, emerging from the mouths of the Dragon, the Animal and the False Prophet. They are diabolical spirits performing wonders and they set out to muster all the kings of the world for battle on the Great Day of God, the Almighty.

So they brought them together to the place called, in Hebrew, Armageddon.*

* Verse 16 has been put immediately before verse 15, which seems to be its natural place.

The words in the background 16:15

"See, I am coming like a thief! Happy is the man who stays awake and keeps his clothes at his side, so that he will not have to walk naked and men see his shame."

The seventh bowl: devastation from the air 16:17

The seventh angel emptied his bowl into the air. A loud voice came out of the Temple, from the Throne, saying,

"The End has come!"

Then followed flashes of lightning, noises and peals of thunder. There was a terrific earthquake, the like of which no man has ever seen since mankind began to live upon the earth—so great and tremendous was this earthquake. The Great City was split into three parts, and the cities of all the nations fell in ruins. And God called to mind Babylon the Great and made her drink the cup of the wine of His furious wrath. Every island fled and the mountains vanished. Great hailstones like heavy weights fell from the sky, and men blasphemed God for the curse of the hail, for it fell upon them with savage and fearful blows.

The judgment of the evil woman announced 17:1

Then came one of the seven angels who held the seven bowls, and said to me,

"Come, and I will show you the judgment passed upon the great Harlot who is seated upon many waters. It is with her that the kings of the earth have debauched themselves and the inhabitants of the earth have become drunk on the wine of her filthiness."

The gorgeous mother of evil 17:3

Then he carried me away in spirit into the desert. There I saw a Woman riding upon a scarlet Animal, covered with blasphemous titles and having seven heads and ten horns. The Woman herself was dressed in purple and scarlet, glittering with gold, jewels and pearls. In her hand she held a golden cup full of the earth's filthiness and her own foul impurity. On her forehead is written a name with a secret meaning—BABYLON THE GREAT, MOTHER OF ALL HARLOTS AND OF THE EARTH'S ABOMINATIONS.

The vision explained 17:6

Then I noticed that the Woman was drunk with the blood of the saints and of the martyrs for Jesus. As I watched her, I was filled with utter amazement, but the angel said to me,

"Why are you amazed? I will explain to you the mystery of the Woman and of the Animal with seven heads and ten horns which carries her. The Animal, which you saw, once lived but now is no more—it will come up out of the Pit only to meet with destruction. The inhabitants of the earth, whose names have not been written in the Book of Life from the foundation of the world, will be utterly astonished when they see that the Animal was, and is not, and yet is to come. (Here we need a mind with understanding.)

"The seven heads are seven hills on which the Woman takes her seat. There are also seven kings; five have been dethroned, one reigns and the other has not yet appeared—when he comes he must remain only for a short time. As for the Animal which once lived but now lives no longer, it is an eighth king which belongs to the seven, but it goes to utter destruction. The ten horns which you saw are ten kings who have not yet received their power to reign, but they will receive authority to be kings for one hour in company with the Animal. They are of one mind, and they will hand over their power and authority to the Animal. They will all go to war with the Lamb, and the Lamb, with His called, chosen and faithful followers, will conquer them. For He is Lord of lords and King of kings."

Then he said to me,

"As for the waters which you saw, on which the Woman took her seat, they are peoples and vast crowds, nations and languages. The ten horns and the Animal which you saw will loathe the Harlot, and leave her deserted and naked. Moreover, they will devour her flesh, and then consume her with fire. For God has put it into their hearts to carry out His Purpose by making them of one mind, and by handing over their authority to the Animal, until the Words of God have been fulfilled.

"The Woman that you saw is the Great City which dominates the kings of the earth."

The final overthrow of Babylon 18:1

Later I saw another angel coming down from Heaven, armed with great authority. The earth shone with the splendour of his presence, and he cried in a mighty voice,

"Fallen, fallen is Babylon* the Great! She has become a haunt of devils, a prison for every unclean spirit, and a cage for every filthy and hateful bird. For all nations have drunk the wine of her passionate unfaithfulness and have fallen thereby. The kings of the earth have debauched themselves with

* Referring to Rome, but prophetically to any great, prosperous but Godless city.

her, and the merchants of the earth have grown rich from the extravagance of her dissipation!"

Then I heard another voice from Heaven, crying,

"Come out from her, O my people, lest you become accomplices in her sins and must share in her punishment. For her sins have mounted up to the sky, and God has remembered the tale of her wickedness. Pay her back in her own coin—yes, pay her back double for all that she has done! In the cup which she mixed for others mix her a drink of double strength! For the pride in which she flaunted herself give her torture and misery! Because she says to herself, 'Here I sit a queen on a throne; I am no woman who lacks a man and I shall never know sorrow!' So in a single day her punishments shall strike her—death, sorrow and famine, and she shall be burned in the fire. For mighty is the Lord God Who judges her!"

The lament over the city 18:9

Then the kings of the earth, who debauched and indulged themselves with her, will wail and lament over her. Standing at a safe distance through very fear of her torment, they will watch the smoke of her burning and cry,

"Alas, alas for the Great City, Babylon the mighty City, that your judgment should come in a single hour."

The merchants of the earth shall also wail and

lament over her, for there is no one left to buy their goods—cargoes of gold and silver, jewels and pearls, fine linen, purple, silk and scarlet, all kinds of scented wood, every sort of ivory vessel, every kind of vessel of precious wood, of bronze, iron and marble; cinnamon, spice, incense, myrrh, frankincense, wine, oil, fine flour and corn; cattle, sheep and horses; chariots, slaves, the very souls of men.

18:15*

Those who brought and sold these things, who had gained their wealth from her, will stand afar off through fear of her punishment, weeping and lamenting and saying,

"Alas, alas for the Great City that was dressed in fine linen, purple and scarlet, and was bedecked with gold and jewels and pearls—alas that in a single hour all that wealth should be destroyed!"

Then every shipmaster and seafarer—sailors and all whose business is upon the sea—stood and watched the smoke of her burning from afar, and cried out,

"What city was ever like the Great City?"

They even threw dust on their heads and cried aloud as they wept, saying,

"Alas, alas for the Great City where all who had ships on the sea grew wealthy through the richness of her treasure! Alas that in a single hour she should be ruined!"

* Verse 14 has been incorporated into verse 23, which seems to be ts natural place.

A comment in the background 18:20

"Rejoice over her fate, O Heaven, and all you saints, apostles and prophets! For God has pronounced His Judgment for you against her!"

The words of Babylon's doom 18:21

Then a mighty angel lifted up a stone like a huge millstone and hurled it into the sea, saying,

"So shall Babylon the Great City be sent hurtling down to disappear for ever! Never more shall the sound of harpists and musicians, flute-players and trumpeters be heard in you again! Never again shall a craftsman of any craft be found in you; never again will the sound of the millstone's grinding be heard in you! No light of a lamp shall ever shine in you again, and the voices of bridegroom and bride shall be heard in you no more! The fruit of your soul's desire is lost to you for ever. All your luxuries and brilliance are lost to you and men will never find them in you again!

"For your merchants were the great ones of the earth, and all nations were seduced by your witchery!"

For in her was discovered the blood of prophets and saints, indeed the blood of all who were ever slaughtered upon the earth.

Rejoicing in Heaven 19:1

Afterwards I heard what sounded like the mighty roar of a vast crowd in Heaven, crying,

"Alleluia! Salvation and Glory and Power belong to our God, for His Judgments are true and just. He has judged the great Harlot who corrupted the earth with her wickedness, and He has avenged upon her the blood of His servants!"

Then they cried a second time,

"Alleluia! The smoke of her destruction ascends for timeless ages!"

Then the twenty-four Elders and the four Living Creatures prostrated themselves and worshipped God Who is seated upon the Throne, saying,

"Amen, Alleluia!"

Then out of the Throne came a voice, saying,

"Praise our God, all you who serve Him, all you who reverence Him, both small and great!"

And then I heard a sound like the voices of a vast crowd, the roar of a great waterfall and the rolling of heavy thunder, and they were saying,

"Alleluia! For the Lord our God, the Almighty, has come into His Kingdom! Let us rejoice, let us be glad with all our hearts. Let us give Him the glory, for the Wedding-day of the Lamb has come, and His Bride has made herself ready. She may be seen dressed in linen, gleaming and spotless—for such linen is the righteous living of the saints!"

Instruction to John 19:9

Then he said to me,

"Write this down: Happy are those who are invited to the Wedding-feast of the Lamb!"

Then he added,

"These are true words of God."

At that I fell at his feet to worship him, but he said to me,

"No! I am your fellow-servant and fellow-servant with your brothers who are holding fast their witness to Jesus. Give your worship to God!"

(This witness to Jesus inspires all prophecy.)

The word of God on the white horse 19:11

Then I saw Heaven wide open, and before my eyes appeared a white horse, whose rider is called Faithful and True, for His judgment and His warfare are just. His eyes are a flame of fire and there are many diadems upon His head. There is a Name written upon Him, known only to himself. He is dressed in a cloak dipped in blood, and the Name by which He is known is the Word of God.

The armies of Heaven follow Him, riding upon white horses and clad in white and spotless linen. Out of His mouth there comes a sharp sword with which to strike the nations. He will shepherd them "with a rod of iron", and alone He will tread the winepress of the furious wrath of God the Almighty. Written upon His cloak and upon His thigh is the Name, KING OF KINGS AND LORD OF LORDS.

The feast of death after battle 19:17

Then I saw an angel standing alone in the blazing light of the sun, and he shouted in a loud voice, calling to all the birds flying in mid-air, "Come, flock together to God's great feast! Here you may eat the flesh of kings and captains, the flesh of strong men, of horses and their riders—the flesh of all men, free men and slaves, small and great!"

And I saw the Animal with the kings of the earth and their armies massed together for battle against the Rider upon the horse and His army. The Animal was captured and with it the False Prophet who had performed marvels in its presence, which he had used to deceive those who accepted the mark of the Animal and worshipped its statue. These two were thrown alive into the Lake of Fire which burns with sulphur.

The rest were killed by the sword which issues from the mouth of the Rider upon the horse; and all the birds gorged themselves on their flesh.

Satan bound for a thousand years 20:1

Then I saw an angel coming down from Heaven with the key of the Pit and a huge chain in his hand. He seized the Dragon, the Serpent of ancient days, who is both the Devil and Satan, and bound him fast for a thousand years. Then he hurled him into the Pit, and locked and sealed it over his head, so that he could deceive the nations no more until the thousand years were past. But then he must be set free for a little while.

The first resurrection 20:4

And I saw thrones, with appointed judges seated upon them. Then I saw the souls of those who had been executed for their witness to Jesus and for proclaiming the Word of God—those who never worshipped the Animal or its statue, and had not accepted its mark upon their foreheads or their hands. They came to life and reigned with Christ for a thousand years. (The rest of the dead did not come to life until the thousand years were over.) This is the First Resurrection. Happy and holy is the one who shares in the First Resurrection! The Second Death cannot touch such men; they shall be priests of God and of Christ, and shall reign with Him for the thousand years.

Satan finally destroyed 20:7

Then, when the thousand years are over, Satan will be released from his prison, and will set out to deceive the nations in the four corners of the earth, Gog and Magog, and to lead them into battle. They will be as numerous as the sand of the seashore.

They came up and spread over the breadth of the earth; they encircled the army of the saints defending the Beloved City. But fire came down from the sky and consumed them. The Devil who deceived them was hurled into the Lake of Fire and Sulphur to join the Animal and the False Prophet. And there they shall be tortured day and night for timeless ages.

The final judgment 20:11

And then I saw a great white Throne, and One seated upon it from Whose Presence both earth and sky fled and vanished.

Then I saw the dead, great and small, standing before the Throne and the books were opened. And another book was opened, which is the Book of Life. And the dead were judged by what was written in the books concerning what they had done. The sea gave up its dead, and Death and the Grave gave up the dead which were in them. And men were judged, each according to what he had done.

Then Death and the Grave were themselves hurled into the Lake of Fire, which is the Second Death. If anyone's name was not found written in the Book of Life he was thrown into the Lake of Fire.

All things made new 21:1

Then I saw a new Heaven and a new earth, for the first Heaven and the first earth had disappeared and the sea was no more. I saw the Holy City, the New Jerusalem, descending from God out of Heaven, prepared as a Bride dressed in beauty for her husband. Then I heard a great voice from the Throne crying,

"See! The Home of God is with men, and He will live among them. They shall be His people, and God Himself shall be with them, and will wipe away every tear from their eyes. Death shall be no more, and never again shall there be sorrow or crying or pain. For all those former things are past and gone."

Then He Who is seated upon the Throne said,

"See, I am making all things new!"

And He added,

"Write this down, for my words are true and to be trusted."

Then He said to me,

"It is done! I am Alpha and Omega, the Beginning and the End. I will give to the thirsty water without price from the Fountain of Life. The victorious shall inherit these things, and I will be God to him and he will be son to Me. But as for the cowards, the faithless and the corrupt, the murderers, the traffickers in sex and sorcery, the worshippers of idols and all liars—their inheritance is in the Lake which burns with fire and sulphur, which is the Second Death."

The vision of the new Jerusalem 21:9

Then one of the seven angels who hold the seven bowls which were filled with the seven last plagues, came to me and said,

"Come, and I will show you the Bride, the Wife of the Lamb."

Then he carried me away in spirit to the top of a vast mountain, and pointed out to me the City, the Holy Jerusalem, descending from God out of Heaven, radiant with the glory of God. Her brilliance sparkled like a very precious jewel with the clear light of crystal. Around her she had a vast and lofty wall in which were twelve gateways with twelve angels at the gates. There were twelve names inscribed over the twelve gateways, and they are the names of the twelve tribes of the sons of Israel. On the east there were three gateways, on the north three gateways, on the south three gateways and on the west three gateways. The wall of the City had twelve foundation-stones, and on these were engraved the names of the twelve Apostles of the Lamb.

The measurement of the city 21:15

The one who was talking to me had a golden rod in his hand with which to measure the City, its gateways and its wall. The City lies foursquare, its length equal to its breadth. He measured the City with his rod and it was twelve thousand furlongs in each direction, for its length, breadth and height are all equal. Then he measured its wall, and found that to be one hundred and forty-four half-yards high by human measurement, (which the angel was using).

The splendour of the city's building 21:18

The wall itself was built of translucent stone, while the City was of purest gold, with the brilliance of glass. The foundation-stones of the wall of the City were fashioned out of every kind of precious stone. The first foundation-stone was jasper, the second sapphire, the third agate, the fourth emerald, the fifth onyx, the sixth cornelian, the seventh goldstone, the eighth beryl, the ninth topaz, the tenth green goldstone, the eleventh zircon, and the twelfth amethyst. The twelve gates were twelve pearls, each gate made of a single pearl. The street of the City was purest gold gleaming like glass.

The splendour within the city 21:22

I could see no Temple in the City, for the Lord, the Almighty God, and the Lamb are Themselves its Temple. The City has no need for the light of sun or moon, for the splendour of God fills it with light and its radiance is the Lamb. The nations will walk by its light, and the kings of the earth will bring their glory into it. The City's gates shall stand open day after day—and there will be no night there. Into the City they will bring the splendours and honours of the nations.

But nothing unclean, no one who deals in filthiness and lies, shall ever at any time enter it—only those whose names are written in the Lamb's Book of Life.

A further glimpse of the city 22:1

Then he showed me the river of the Water of Life, sparkling like crystal as it flowed from the Throne of God and of the Lamb. In the middle of the street of the City and on either bank of the river grew the Tree of Life, bearing twelve fruits, a different kind for each month. The leaves of the Tree were for the healing of the nations.

Nothing that has cursed mankind shall exist any

longer; the Throne of God and of the Lamb shall be within the City. His servants shall worship Him; they shall see His Face, and His Name will be upon their foreheads. Night shall be no more; they have no more need for either lamplight or sunlight, for the Lord God will shed His Light upon them and they shall reign as kings for timeless ages.

The Angel endorses the revelation 22:6

Then the angel said to me,

"These words are true and to be trusted, for the Lord God, Who inspired the prophets, has sent His angel to show His servants what must shortly happen.

"See, I come quickly! Happy is the man who pays heed to the words of the prophecy in this book."

John's personal endorsement 22:8

It is I, John, who have heard and seen these things. At the time when I heard and saw them I fell at the feet of the angel who showed them to me and I was about to worship him. But he said to me,

"No! I am fellow-servant to you and to your brothers, to the prophets and to those who keep the words of this book. Give your worship to God!"

Then he added,

"Do not seal up the words of the prophecy in this

book, for the time of their fulfilment is near. Let the wicked man continue his wickedness and the filthy man his filthiness; let the good man continue his good deeds, and the holy man continue in holiness."

The interjected words of Christ 22:12

"See, I come quickly! I carry My reward with me, and repay every man according to his deeds. I am Alpha and Omega, the First and the Last, the Beginning and the End. Happy are those who wash their robes, for they have the right to the Tree of Life and the freedom of the gates of the City. Shut out from the City shall be the depraved, the sorcerers, the impure, the murderers and the idolaters, and everyone who loves and practises a lie!

"I, Jesus, have sent my angel to you with this Testimony for the Churches. I am both the Root and Stock of David, and the bright Star of the morning!"

The invitation of the church and the spirit 22:17

The Spirit and the Bride say, "Come!"
Let everyone who hears this also say, "Come!"
Let the thirsty man come, and let everyone who wishes take the Water of Life as a gift.

John's testimony to this book 22:18

Now I bear solemn witness to every man who hears the words of prophecy in this book:

If anyone adds to these words God will add to him the disasters described in this book; if anyone takes away from the words of prophecy in this book, God will take away from him his share in the Tree of Life and in the Holy City which are described in this book.

He, Who is Witness to all this, says,

"Yes, I am coming very quickly!"

"Amen, come, Lord Jesus!"

The grace of the Lord Jesus be with all His people.

ON TRANSLATING THE NEW TESTAMENT

Since this is the last of the four New Testament "books" which I have translated, it has been suggested that readers might be interested to know something of the principles which underly my interpretation of the original Greek Text.

It is not enough merely to replace outmoded words with their modern equivalents, and in any case the result of that kind of process is liable to be a strange and unlovely hybrid language. We must be much more fundamental than that; we have to go right back to the comparatively workaday Greek of the New Testament documents themselves and translate them afresh, not into slang, but into vigorous contemporary English. It has never been my object to denigrate the majesty and beauty of the Authorized Version, which is indeed incomparable. I have rather sought to rescue tremendous and inspiring truths from what is sometimes a familiar prison of traditional beauty.

Fifteen years have proved to me that this is an exceedingly difficult task. I do not myself believe that there is any such thing as "timeless English", and the very best that a translator can do is to make the message and burden of what he translates urgent and contemporary to his own generation. And in attempting to do this I have of course had far more information and scholarship available to me than the translators of 1611 ever possessed.

It will be obvious that my particular method of translation is more appropriate, and indeed more necessary, in some cases than in others. For example, as I wrote in the

Preface to this present volume, I have not attempted to interpret the high poetry of John's vision. But, at the other end of the scale, there was plenty of room for interpretative translation if one was to reveal the force and relevance of, say, Paul's epistles.

In the following notes, I have described some of my tools, and how and why I have wielded them. But behind all my work, a great deal of which was done amidst the busyness of parochial duties, I have always been aware of one pressing question: How can the Christian Faith capture the minds and hearts of men of today and tomorrow if it is always and everywhere proclaimed in the language of a bygone age? It seems to me only too probable that where language is consistently archaic, people, and especially young people, will assume that Christianity itself is obsolete.

1960 *J. B. Phillips*

THE SEEDS of my desire to translate or interpret were sown, I think, in my early boyhood. I still remember my childish exasperation at "churchy" or archaic language in liturgy, sermons and hymns. It seemed to me that matters of positive fact were being described as a sort of celestial fairy tale. I was irritated, I think, because if these matters of which the parsons spoke were true, I felt intuitively that we were in the presence of things, and indeed of a Person, more awe-inspiring as well as more real than anything that existed, even in the sunlit world of childhood. It struck me as monstrous that the Truth which lay behind the appearance of things should be dimmed and distorted by the wrong voice and the wrong language. It was not long before I began translating almost automatically for myself, although it was a great many years before I began to translate for the benefit of anyone else!

It was my late headmaster, Shirley Goodwin, a scholar of Balliol College, Oxford, who some years later first taught me the meaning of translation. In the sixth form at Emanuel School, London, we came under his direct tuition. In his gentlemanly way he assumed (quite wrongly for most of us), that we had already mastered all the vagaries of grammar and syntax in Latin and Greek. He urbanely supposed that we, who were soon to go up to Oxford or Cambridge, need no longer be bothered with the vulgar mechanics of these two dead but magnificent languages, and with a fine infectious enthusiasm he taught us to enjoy the Classics. Above all he taught us really to translate. "Cribs", that is, translations, were not forbidden to us sixth-formers, but how we learned to criticize, and even to despise those who merely substituted English equivalents for Greek or Latin words! We learned to hate "translator's English" more than the Devil himself! We would spend a whole morning on a single verse of an Ode of Horace, searching for the *mot juste* or the phrase with precisely the right flavour. And if this was not very useful to us for the purpose of passing examinations, it gave us a lasting insight into what is and what is not real translation.

In the years that followed my Ordination in 1930, apart from constant efforts at simplification, and trying to act on the principle "never use a long word where a short one will do", there was little opportunity in parochial life for attempts at translation. Like many other priests in the Church of England I did my best within the existing liturgical framework to make Services as real as possible, and to keep sermons free from technical jargon. But, again like many others, I was continually haunted by the thought that the fine old words of Cranmer and his contemporaries were meaning little or nothing to the occasional Churchgoer. The regular member, or so I comforted myself, was probably translating as he went along, but to the majority of parents who brought their children to be baptised, what could such words as "whosoever is here dedicated to thee by our office and ministry" possibly mean—especially in a bureaucratic age?

But the actual work of translating the New Testament came about almost accidentally, and no one is more surprised than I am that what was begun as a small private venture should have brought me appreciation from many parts of the English-speaking world. Briefly the story is this. During the War, when I was Vicar of The Good Shepherd, Lee, in the South-east of London, I was in charge of a flourishing group of young people. We had had, and were to have, our share of bombing and the usual discomforts of war. At the close of the Youth Club's evening activities I used to read some verses of Paul's epistles. After all, I thought to myself, much of this was written by one Christian in difficulty to other Christians in difficulty, and surely these young people will find them appropriate to their situation. But I was met by polite but complete lack of comprehension! These youngsters, who were by no means unintelligent, simply did not understand "Bible language". All my old passion for making truth comprehensible, and all my desire to do a bit of real translation, urged me to put some relevant New Testament truths into language which these young people could understand. This I did, and was rewarded beyond my expectations as they realised for the first time, not merely that the epistles of Paul really could make sense, but that the inspired words were extremely relevant to life as they knew it.

Then followed a strange accident. Moved by admiration for his Christian insight, I wrote to Dr. C. S. Lewis at Oxford, and sent him a copy of my version of Paul's letter to Colossae. He wrote back as follows:

> "Thank you a hundred times. I thought I knew Colossians pretty well but your paraphrase makes it far more significant, it was like seeing a familiar picture after it's been cleaned . . . I hope very much you will carry out your plan of doing all the epistles . . ."

What greater encouragement could I want? Here was a first-rate scholar with infinitely more knowledge of both the Classics and present-day English than I myself possess encouraging me to "do the lot"! Naturally it was no easy task, especially in war-time. Those who lived in any big city in Britain will know what sort of times we lived through. Perhaps only they will know how difficult it was to concentrate, and will appreciate why I always kept a copy of the work as it proceeded in as bombproof a place as possible! Then came the difficulty of finding a publisher. One after another returned the work, which was a translation of the New Testament epistles only, remarking politely that there were already good modern translations in existence. But at last Dr. C. S. Lewis' publisher,

Mr. Geoffrey Bles, agreed to accept the work for publication and to my very great joy Dr. Lewis agreed to write a Foreword and what is more, presented me with what I think is an admirable title, *Letters to Young Churches*.

The essential principles of translation

There seem to me to be three necessary tests which any work of transference from one language to another must pass before it can be classed as good translation. The first is simply that it must not sound like a translation at all. If it is skilfully done, and we are not previously informed, we should be quite unaware that it *is* a translation, even though the work we are reading is far distant from us in both time and place. That is a first, and indeed essential test, but it is not by itself sufficient. For the translator himself may be a skilful writer, and although he may have conveyed the essential meaning, characterisation and plot of the original author, he may have so strong a style of his own that he has completely changed that of the original author. The example of this kind of translation which springs most readily to mind is Fitzgerald's *Rubáiyát of Omar Khayyám*. I would therefore make this the second test: that a translator does his work with the least possible obtrusion of his own personality. The third and final test which a good translator should be able to pass is that of being able to produce in the hearts and minds of his readers an effect equivalent to that produced by the author upon his original readers. Of course no translator living would claim that his work successfully achieves these three ideals. But he must bear them in mind constantly as principles for his guidance.

Translation as interpretation

I have often been told that my own translation work is more of a "paraphrase" or "interpretation" than a real translation. While I feel that this is not altogether true, this seems to me to be the right place to set down a justification for my methods. As I have frequently said, a translator is not a commentator. He is usually well aware of the different connotations which a certain passage may bear, but unless his work is to be cluttered with footnotes he is bound, after careful consideration, to set down what is the most likely meaning. Occasionally one is driven into what appears to be a paraphrase, simply because a literal translation of the Greek would prove unintelligible. But where this has proved necessary I have always been careful to avoid giving any slant or flavour which is purely of my own making. That is why I have been rather reluctant to accept the suggestion that my translations are "interpretations"! If the word interpretation is used in a bad sense, that is, if it is meant that a work is tendentious, or that there has been a manipulation of the words of New

Testament Scripture to fit some private point of view, then I would still strongly repudiate the charge! But "interpretation" can also mean transmitting meaning from one language to another, and skilled interpreters in world affairs do not intentionally inject any meaning of their own. In this sense I gladly accept the word interpretation to describe my work. For, as I see it, the translator's function is to understand as fully and deeply as possible what the New Testament writers had to say and then, after a process of what might be called reflective digestion, to write it down in the language of people today. And here I must say that it is essential for the interpreter to know the language of both parties. He may be a first-class scholar in New Testament Greek and know the significance of every traditional crux, and yet be abysmally ignorant of how his contemporaries outside his scholastic world are thinking and feeling.

Words and their context

After reading a large number of commentaries I have a feeling that some scholars, at least, have lived so close to their Greek Testaments that they have forgotten their sense of proportion. I doubt very much whether the New Testament writers were as subtle or as self-conscious as some commentators would make them appear. For the most part I am convinced that they had no idea that they were writing Holy Scripture. They would be, or indeed perhaps are, amazed to learn what meanings are sometimes read back into their simple utterances! Paul, for instance, writing in haste and urgency to some of his wayward and difficult Christians, was not tremendously concerned about dotting the 'i's and crossing the 't's of his message. I doubt very much whether he was even concerned with being completely consistent with what he had already written. Consequently, it seems to me quite beside the point to study his writings microscopically, as it were, and deduce hidden meanings of which almost certainly he was quite unaware. His letters are alive, and moving in both senses of that word, and their meaning can no more be appreciated by cold minute examination than can the real beauty of a bird's flight be appreciated by dissection after its death. We have to take these living New Testament documents in their context, a context of supreme urgency and often of acute danger. Far too often have I read of the use of a certain word in the New Testament as though the various writers from Matthew to John the Divine had met in committee and decided precisely on its vocabulary and its meaning! But a word is modified very considerably by the context in which it appears, and if a translator fails to realise this, we are not far away from the electronic word transmuter. The translators of the Authorised Version were certainly not unaware of this modification, even though they had such extreme reverence for the actual words of Holy Writ. Three hundred years ago they did not hesitate to translate the Greek word EKBALLO by such varying expressions as *put out*, *drive out*, *bring forth*, *send out*, *tear out*, *take out*, *leave out*, *cast out*, etc., basing their decision on the context. And as an example of this translational freedom, we read in Matthew 27:44 that the thieves who were crucified with Jesus "cast the same in his teeth", where the Greek word simply means "abused him".

The translator must be flexible

I feel strongly that a translator, although he must make himself as familiar as possible with New Testament Greek usage, must steadfastly refuse to be driven by the bogey of consistency. He must be guided both by the context in which a word appears, and by the sensibilities of modern English readers. In the story of the raising of Lazarus, for example, Martha's objection to opening the grave would be natural enough to an Eastern mind. But to put into her lips the words, "by this time he's stinking", would sound to Western ears unpleasantly out of key with the rest of that moving story. Similarly, we know that the early Christians greeted one another with "an holy kiss". Yet to introduce such an expression into a modern English translation immediately reveals the gulf between the early Christians and ourselves, the very thing which I as a translator am trying to bridge. Again, it is perfectly true, if we are to translate literally, that Jesus said, "Blessed are the beggars in spirit". In an Eastern land, where the disparity between rich and poor was very great, beggars were common. But it is to my mind extremely doubtful whether the word "beggar" in our Welfare State, or indeed in most English-speaking countries, conjures up the mental image which Jesus intended to convey to his hearers. It was not the social misfit or the work-shy, spiritually speaking, but the one who was obviously and consciously in need whom Jesus describes as "blessed" or "happy".

The use of insight and sympathy

Perhaps a few words about the kind of technique which I have adopted may be introduced here. I have found imaginative sympathy, not so much with words as with people, to be essential. If it is not presumptuous to say so, I attempted, as far as I could, to think myself into the heart and mind of Paul, for example, or of Mark or of John the Divine. Then I tried further to imagine myself as each of the New Testament authors writing his particular message for the people of today. No one could succeed in doing this superlatively well, if only because of the scantiness of our knowledge of the first century A.D. But this has been my ideal, and that is why consistency and meticulous accuracy have sometimes both been sacrificed in the attempt to transmit freshness and life across the centuries.

The cross-headings which appear throughout the translation are meant to make it both more readable and more intelligible; at the same time they are intended to be quite unobtrusive and can easily be ignored. But by the use of these headings solid and rather forbidding slabs of continuous writing (such as appear in the Greek Text), are made more assimilable to the modern reader, whose reading habits have already been "conditioned" by the comparatively recent usage of clear punctuation, intelligent paragraphing and good printer's type.